The W

The first play in D. C. Jackson's 'Stewarton Trilogy'
for Borderline Theatre Company, *The Wall*, won
the Best Ensemble at the 2007–8 Critics' Awards
for Theatre in Scotland and was shortlisted for the
Saltire Society/Royal Mail Scottish First Book of the
Year Award. It was followed by *The Ducky* in 2009.
The Chooky Brae completes the trilogy in 2010.
My Romantic History was staged earlier in the same
year by the Bush Theatre and Sheffield Crucible.
He has also had short plays produced by Oran Mor
(*Matinee Idle*, *Drawing Bored*, *Out on the Wing* and
Company Policy) and the Arches Theatre Company
(*Hello*, part of *Spend a Penny*). He was the Pearson
Writer in Residence at the Royal Court for 2008.

D C JACKSON

The Wall

faber and faber

First published Great Britain in 2008
by Faber and Faber Limited
Bloomsbury House, 74-77 Great Russell Street, London WC1 8 3DA

Typeset by Country Setting, Kingsdown, Kent CT14 8ES
Printed and bound by CPI Group (UK) Ltd, Croydon, CR0 4YY

A CIP record for this book
is available from the British Library

ISBN 978-0-571-24229-0

The Wall, presented by Borderline Theatre Company, Ayr, in association with the Tron Theatre, Glasgow, was first performed at the Tron Theatre on 28 February 2008. The cast was as follows:

Barry Scott Hoatson
Michelle Kirstin McLean
Rab Finn Den Hertog
Norma Sally Reid

Director Gregory Thompson
Designer Becky Minto
Lighting Designer Lizzie Powell
Stage Manager Jacqui Howard
Deputy Stage Manager Carrie Taylor
Deputy Stage Manager Anne E. Page
Wardrobe Supervisor Jennie Loof
Producer Eddie Jackson

Acknowledgements

This play was only made possible because of the help and assistance of a number of people. Firstly Liz Lochhead: she has been my inspiration, champion and friend. I heard a great quote attributed to Jack Lemmon, although I'm not sure who first coined it: 'If you're lucky enough to reach the top floor it is only right to send down the elevator for the next person.' Liz certainly has.

Special praise to John Tiffany, who has been unfailingly generous, helpful and kind. Thanks are also due to Julie Ellen, Caroline Newall, David Grieg, Nicola McCartney, Clare Dow and everyone at the Playwright's Studio Scotland as well as the staff of Borderline Theatre and the Tron.

There have been quite a few actors and directors who have participated in the development of *The Wall*, but none deserve more thanks or acknowledgement than Leah MacRae. Her talent and enthusiasm knew no bounds. The others (Johnny Austin, Sally Reid, Mark Wood, James McKenzie, Matthew McVarish, Kieran Hurley, Sharon Osdin, Neil Campbell, Scott Hoatson, Kirstin McLean, Maryam Hamidi, Steve Collins, Liam Hurley and Adrian Osmond) have also been exceptionally kind, and their help gave me the confidence to finish the play.

If this is a play about a dysfunctional family, then I could not have hoped to have a more functional one. Edward, Jacqueline and Ben have put up with a lot from me over the years and I owe them a huge debt. I am very lucky.

Finally I must acknowledge my friend Andrew Milne, who originally told me about the wanking monkeys.

D C Jackson, Glasgow, February 2008

THE WALL

Act One

SCENE ONE

Sunday afternoon, August 2005: the wall.
Barry is seventeen. He is sitting alone on the wall, reading a book without a cover. Michelle, a fifteen-year-old goth, enters. She stands a little away, watching him. Becoming aware of her, Barry puts his book down.

Barry Are you lost?

Michelle What? No.

Barry You look lost.

Michelle I was going to sit on the wall.

Barry Oh aye? You're not lost then – here, it's here.

Michelle I didn't think there would be anyone sitting on it.

Barry Life's full of surprises like that.

Michelle Yeah . . .

Barry It's a big wall.

Michelle What?

Barry It's a big wall, not as big as the Great Wall of China, say, that's a great big wall, but this is a big wall. You can join me and we can both sit on the wall.

Michelle Maybe I wanted to be on my own.

Barry Well, I'm not leaving, I'm not forcing you to leave, but I'm not leaving.

Michelle I'll just go.

Barry dismounts the wall and stands with Michelle.

Barry You don't have to leave. The two of us can sit here peacefully and co-exist on the wall and not even acknowledge the other. We can pretend we're on a bus. Look.

He jumps back on the wall, opens his book and starts reading again. After a moment Michelle hauls herself onto the wall. They sit together, affecting ignoring each other but stealing glances.

You on your summer holidays?

Michelle Yeah.

Barry Summer holidays are the best, ay? Not a care in the world.

Michelle shoots him a stare that indicates she has every care in the world.

Michelle I hate the holidays.

Barry Good for you, you like school. That's great.

Michelle I fucking hate school. I hate the fucking holidays because they always end back at fucking school.

Barry Oh well. Be over before you know it. Funny that. Isn't it? The holidays, so much happens and it all happens so fast. It's over before you know it. Like a microwave. The holidays are like a microwave. I was the same. I liked the holidays but I was the same.

Michelle I thought we're pretending we're on the bus.

Barry I'm just making conversation to help pass the journey.

Michelle I'll move seats.

Barry Fine.

He opens his book again.

Michelle You're Norma Gordon's big brother, aren't you?

Barry Barry.

Michelle So do you think you've passed your Highers this time, Barry?

Barry What do you mean, 'this time'?

Michelle Well, you failed them last year, didn't you?

Barry What? Was it in the *Kilmarnock Standard*? How come everyone in Stewarton knows what I got for my Highers?

Michelle Because it's Stewarton. It's not like we live in Glasgow. Or Kilmarnock. Or anything. Your dad comes into my mum's shop. He's quite a character, your dad. He didn't say it like he was disappointed or anything either, he said that it 'showed how fallible standardised testing is'. There's always this year's, anyway.

Barry You're Michelle Montgomery, aren't you?

Michelle Yeah.

Barry I think my dad might have gone out with your mum.

Michelle He what?!

Barry God, sorry. I always say the wrong thing. This was before my mum and your dad obviously. When they were younger.

Michelle I don't think so. Your dad's ancient, Barry. I mean, he's older. He's older than my mum. My mum's actually dead young. She just looks old cos she wears organic clothing. They couldn't have gone out when they were younger because they weren't younger together.

A pause.

Barry Sorry, I didn't mean anything . . .

Silence.

Michelle It's fine. Let's just get back on the bus.

Barry fidgets.

Barry Look, I'm really sorry. I didn't think. I cannae tell what age grown-ups are. She used to give me aniseed balls when I went in your shop. I always liked going into the health-food shop. Except when old Alice was working. She always gave me evils. Does she live with you or something?

Michelle Yeah. She's moving out, though. She's bought a bungalow. They make me call her aunt. Aunt Alice. She isn't my aunt, though.

Barry I've got an aunt like that. Aunt Valerie. She always gives me twenty quid at Christmas but, so I don't mind. More than I get off my real aunt and uncle.

Michelle Aunt Alice always gives me a shite Christmas. Books. Books and underwear.

Barry Books are a good present. What kind of books?

Michelle Boring ones. Last year she gave me this one about oranges.

Barry Oranges?

Michelle *Oranges Are Not the Only Fruit*, I think it was. I haven't read it.

Barry Old Alice is full of surprises.

Michelle Not really. I've known her like the whole of my life and the only surprising thing she's ever done is buy a bungalow.

Pause.

Barry So she must be a bit like your dad, then . . .

Michelle What?

Barry Oh God, sorry, I didn't mean, I only mean that . . .
I . . . you . . . don't have a dad, and she lives with you
and . . . I mean, oh God. Look I'm really sorry.

Pause.

Anyway there's not much difference between my dad and
having no dad anyway . . . Oh God, that's a stupid thing
to say . . .

I don't know anything about your dad, I know saying
that probably makes you suspect I do know something
about your dad, but I don't know anything. I don't even
know if there's a something to know. About your dad.
That's why I said I was sorry because I've never heard
anyone mention your dad so I suppose there's probably
a reason for that. And it's probably not a good reason –
I mean, what's a good reason to abandon your daughter?
Not that he necessarily abandoned you. I mean he might
have had a good reason. If he did. (*Beat.*) Or he might be
dead. Sorry. Look, I'm sorry, I didn't mean anything, any
of that . . . Shut up, Barry, shut up shut up. SHUT UP.

Barry dismounts the wall.

I always say the wrong thing. Now you understand why
I failed my Highers and I understand why you want to be
on your own. I'm sorry. I'll leave you alone, I'll go to the
wall beside the Chooky Brae. I shouldn't even be chatting
up wee Michelle Montgomery.

Michelle Was that you chatting me up?

Barry looks sheepish.

You need some practice.

Barry I know. I'm sorry. I'll leave you alone.

Barry begins to exit.

Michelle Tomorrow.

Barry Tomorrow?

Michelle After tea. Maybe I'll let you practise some more. You need to practise.

Barry exits. Michelle is alone for a moment until Norma enters. Norma is fourteen. She dresses in the sports-casual style lazily attributed to neds.

Norma Was that my brother?

Michelle Yeah.

Norma Were you talking to my brother?

Michelle No. A bit. Sort of.

Norma What you doing?

Michelle Nothin'.

Norma How?

Michelle I'm waiting.

Norma How?

Michelle Just by sitting here.

Norma No, but *how* are you waiting?

Michelle I told you. I'm waiting by sitting here preparing for an occurrence. I'm just quietly biding my time in anticipation.

Norma No, but *how* are you waiting?

Michelle Do you mean what's my waiting style or why am I waiting? What am I waiting for?

Norma Aye.

Michelle Van.

Norma How the van?

Michelle My great-gran gave me ten pounds to do her messages this morning.

Norma You're doing your nan's messages at the van? Does your nan just like eat ice cream and crebs all the time?

Michelle I've already done her messages but she doesn't know what anything costs so I always get my fags out her change. And she isn't my nan, she's my great-nan.

Norma That's a sin.

Michelle She knows I keep the change.

Norma She's on a pension.

Michelle She doesn't mind.

Norma It's still a sin but . . . Spending it on fags.

Michelle She smokes. She started smoking when she was twelve.

Norma I've never seen your great-granny smoke.

Michelle Why would you have?

Norma There's nothing going on in Stewarton I don't see. I'm very perceptive.

Michelle She only smokes in the house. She says it's not ladylike to smoke in the outdoors.

Norma What age is your great-gran?

Michelle I don't know.

Norma She must be ancient. She's a great-gran. I don't know anyone else with a great-granny.

Michelle I don't know, I think she's like seventy or eighty.

Norma Coo. What age is your nan?

Michelle I don't know, fifty-something

Norma What age is your mum, then?

Michelle You're right nosey, Norma. Mind your own business.

Norma She must be dead young for a mum, but. You're dead lucky. My mum and dad are ancient. Your great-granny's got a dead glamorous name too.

Michelle Minnie Malloy?

Norma Yeah, 's like an old film star. *Sin in Stewarton*, starring Minnie Malloy. Dead glamorous. I've been round her house with my nan. She called me her wee lamb and she gave me a poke.

Michelle She gave you a poke?

Norma A poke of sweets. Can I get a fag, then?

Michelle No.

Norma How no?

Michelle How?

Norma How no?

Michelle I've not got any fags yet, that's why I'm waiting on the van. Not that I'll give you one when it comes.

Norma Why?

Michelle Bad for you.

Norma Smoking's bad for you too. Bad for everyone.

Michelle How?

Norma Lung diseasies.

Michelle Lung diseasies?

Norma Aye, smoking causes lung diseasies and eczema.

Michelle Eczema?

Norma Aye, it's a pure sin, my Aunt Valerie's got it and it makes her hands all scabby and itchy.

Michelle It's emphysema smoking causes. Smoking causes lung diseasies and emphysema. Lung diseases.

Norma How do you do it, then?

Michelle It's just like whistling. You know how to whistle, don't you kid? You just purse your lips and blow. Except with smoking you suck.

Norma No, *how* do you smoke?

Michelle I just told you how.

Norma You think you're a right smart arse don't you, Michelle Montgomery? I know *how*'s no proper English but you knew what I meant. My dad says it's very important we hold on to our folk culture. He says the English they teach you in school is folking cultural imperialism. My mum says that's how he's no allowed up the school at parents' evening. He wrote them a letter an' I'm allowed to write 'how' in essays now. You shouldnae be smoking at your age, anyhow.

Michelle I'm nearly sixteen.

Norma Is that how you have tae wait on the van? Because 'nearly' isnae? Because Mr Iqbal willnae sell them to you because you're *fifteen*? You shouldnae be smoking at your age.

Michelle I'll be sixteen in a week. You know the first thing I'm going to do? I'll smoke a cigarette right in her face.

Norma Who?

Michelle My Aunt Alice.

Norma Will she no go ballistic?

Michelle How can she? Sixteen's legal. Tony Blair'd given me a light himself.

Norma Tony Blair doesn't smoke.

Michelle No, but I bet he's got a lighter. He'll have to have a lighter so's he can give visiting Europeans a light. They all smoke in Europe.

Norma This is in Europe. Ayrshire's Europe. Stewarton's Europe.

Michelle Everybody here smokes.

Norma I don't smoke.

Michelle You're just by asking me for a fag.

Norma Maybe I wanted it for a joint.

Michelle What age are you?

Norma I'm in the year below you, Michelle, it's not like there's a generation gap. I'm fourteen. Fourteen. Nearly nothing.

Michelle Where did you get hash?

Norma I never said I did have hash, I said maybe I wanted it for a joint.

Michelle Well, do you?

Norma What?

Michelle Want it for a joint?

Norma Maybe.

Michelle So you do have hash?

Norma Maybe.

Michelle So where did you get hash?

Norma I never said I did, smart arse, I said 'maybe'. And anyway, how is it anything to do with Tony Blair if you smoke in your house? Isnae a council house. 'S a private house, isnae anything to do with him.

*The van chimes play. Michelle walks off, followed by
Norma.*

Wait up, Michelle, am I getting a fag or not?

*Rab enters immediately. Rab is sixteen. He is a bam.
He is bouncing a ball as he walks and begins to
bounce it against the wall.*

Rab Right, if I bouncing-catch it a thousand times
without dropping it I'm going straight home for a wank.
If I don't, I go into Iqbal's and ask out Veera Iqbal,
straight out – 'Howzabout it?'

*Rab drops the ball after about twenty bounces, but
starts bouncing again.*

From now.

*Again he only manages a clutch of bounces before
dropping it and starting again.*

Right, this times is for keepsies.

He bounces successfully for a spell.

And maybe only five hunner.

He keeps bouncing until Norma enters.

One hunner. One hunner and one. One hunner and two.
One hunner and three. One hunner and four. One hunner
and five. One hunner and six.
     Alright, Norma, how's it going?

Norma Alright. How's it going?

Rab Alright. What you doing?

Norma Nothing – what you doing?

Rab Nothing. One hunner and seventeen.

Norma You're playing with a ball.

Rab Aye. Here's one, Norma. What do you call a lesbian wi' two arseholes?

Norma I don't know.

Rab PE Department. Haw haw. Better no tell your wee pal Michelle Montgomery that one but.

Norma Why?

Rab Well, old health-food June . . .

Norma What do you mean?

Rab Well, health-food June. She's a bean-muncher.

Norma I know.

Rab Do you, Norma?

Norma Aye, she runs the health-food shop.

Rab No, I mean she's a bean-flicker.

Norma I don't understand.

Rab Have you never heard what they call her?

Norma June the lemon, aye, how?

Rab Well did you never wonder how they called her that?

Norma She runs the health-food shop.

Rab No. She's a lemon, Norma, a bean-flicker, a carpet-muncher, a tuppence-licker. Two hunner and one, two hunner and two . . .

Norma What do you mean, Rab? This isnae funny any more.

Rab She's a bean – a les-bean. She's a lemon, a lezzer, a lesbo. I cannae make it clearer.

   Norma is agog.

Norma No way.

Rab Aye, she's way lesbian. Completely vagatarian. You know the other one out the health-food shop?

Norma Old Alice?

Rab Aye, she's her bird.

Norma No way, Rab, you're talking shit, she's about eighty or something. Old Alice is Liberian? It's aw models and pop stars that are Liberian.

Rab God's honest. Sneaky Pete saw them.

Norma Saw them?

Rab Lezzing.

Norma No way. Sneaky Pete talks shit. There's no gay folk in Stewarton. My dad says it's cos the Bonnet Guild puts something in the water.

Rab God's honest, Norma.

Norma How'd he see them lezzing?

Rab Went in tae nick some crunchy bars and he saw them out the back.

Norma Doing what?

Rab I cannae explain it, but I could lend you some videos.

Norma Gonnae stop playing with the ball while you're talking to me?

Rab Naw. I cannae, Norma, I'm testing myself. Three hunner and one, three hunner and two . . .

Norma Can you roll joints, Rab?

Rab Can I roll joints? Can I roll joints? I'm the big roller, wee Norma. How? Three hunner and fifteen . . .

Norma I've got a bit of hash, but I can't roll joints.

Rab immediately stops bouncing the ball.

Rab Haw haw. Something good always happens when you're down the wall. I love the holidays. Show us it, then.

Norma struggles to remove a small package from her tracksuit trousers. She hands it to Rab, who removes the cannabis and inspects it.

Where did you get it? Off Dugs? Robby Rocket-pants? Stiffy? Slick Rick? You didn't get it off Gonk, did you?

Norma No.

Rab There's only one other person you could have got it off.

Norma *and* **Rab** (*together*) My dad.

Rab I thought you were going to say *my* dad!

Norma Don't tell anyone, but.

Rab I won't.

Norma Serious. He'd literally kill me.

Rab No bother. Does he do a bit, your dad? You know – does he do a bit?

Norma He disnae do any, he just smokes it. He doesn't know I've got it.

Rab Right, so it's a sneaky tax out the big man's stash? No bother, Norma, it's in the vault. Have you got skins?

Norma No. That's all I've got.

Rab I've got fags. Have you got twenty p?

Norma No. That's all I've got.

Rab So I have to buy the skins, donate the skreg and roll it?

Norma Aye.

Rab That's roller's privilege, then baccy privilege, then skin privilege. You only get lasties on the joint, mucker.

Norma Aye, that'll be right.

Rab Serious, Norma. Rules is rules.

Norma Fuck off, Rab.

Rab Go and get the skins, then, here's fifty p. Get the crebs in, too.

Rab hands her fifty p.

Norma Give me the hash back first.

Rab Chill oot, wee Norma, here you go.

Rab offers it to her then snatches it away three times in succession before finally putting it back in his pocket.

Norma doll, where am I going to go? It's Stewarton, I'm no going to bump you, pal. You're asking me a favour. 'Will I roll you a McGuire big banger?' Yes, I will, Norma, but if I'm doing you a wee favour then we're pals and if we're pals then we've got to trust each other, so you go an get the skins and I'll stay here and wait for you.

Norma Aye, right.

Rab Serious. We cannae toke together without a bit of trust. It's an intimacy.

Norma Promise you willnae steal it, Rab.

Rab Promise, pal. I'm trusting you with my ten bob. If I tax it you can keep my ten bob. You didnae pay for it anyhow, did you?

Norma Piss off, Rab.

Rab Chill, Norma, I'll be here. Go. And get. The. Skins.

Norma (*grudgingly*) Alright.

Rab Get Zig-Zags but. Iqbal only sells Swan and Zig-Zag. Swan are shite. I'll wait here.

Norma leaves and Rab starts to bounce the ball against the wall once more.

(*Shouts.*) And get pickled onion Space Raiders!
Right, if I get a thousand bouncy catches before wee Norma gets back I'm going to tax her blow and live life as an outlaw, committing rabberies to get by. All the fannies will aw be like, 'Aw naw, we've been Rabbed, there's been a Rabbery,' and I'll be like, 'Haw haw, get it up aw youse.'
And if I don't, I won't. Just have a wee toke wi wee Norma then go up the shop and ask out Veera Iqbal.

Rab drops the ball after very few bounces.

Oh well. Rules is meant to be broken.

Rab starts to exit.

Right. Home, joint, Champo. Then treat myself like a lady. I love the holidays.

SCENE TWO

Monday evening: the wall.
Michelle is on the wall. She wears full war paint and clothes entirely inappropriate for hanging about the wall on a summer's evening. Goth in a disco. She is waiting for Barry and checks her watch sporadically while adjusting her bustier and reapplying lip-gloss. Eventually she gets up and paces from one end of the wall to the other. After repeating this movement she gives up and exits. Beat. Barry and Rab enter. Barry checks his watch and looks uncomfortable.

18

Barry You still going up the shop, Rab?

Rab How, you walking me?

Barry Eh, no, you're alright, Rab, I'm just going to hang about here.

Rab You wanting me to get you something?

Barry Nah, I'm alright.

Rab You no wanting a wee tin of ginger?

Barry I'm alright.

Rab How d'you no want a wee tin of ginger?

Barry I'm alright.

Rab Aye, I ken you're alright, but you no wanting a wee tin of ginger? I'll crash you. I wouldnae think you were a skadger, Barry man.

Rab mimes taking a can of juice from the fridge, opening and drinking it.

Tsht. Gulp gulp gulp.

Barry I said I'm alright, I'm no thirsty. I said I'm fine, Rab. I'm fine. Are you going up the shop?

Rab Aye, I said I am. You're a right moody cunt, Barry.

Pause.

Is that your wee Norma coming roon the Monkey Trail? Anyways, look, I'm gonnae need to boost the now, Barry, I cannae get you any juice anyhow. No coming back this way. See you round.

Rab exits. Norma enters.

Norma Was that Rab McGuire? I need to talk to him.

Barry Wait a minute, Norma. Why do you need to talk to Rab McGuire?

Norma None of your business, Barry.

Barry Rab McGuire's a bam.

Norma I need to go after him. It's Im. Potent.

Barry I'm really not sure I want you hanging about Rab, Norma.

Norma Well, I'm no sure it's got fuck all to do with you anyway, Barry.

Barry I'm your big brother, Norma.

Norma Ah know, but that disnae mean you can pick my pals.

Michelle enters.

Please can I go, Barry? Please, it's Im. Portant.

Barry On you go. But I want a word with you later.

Norma exits, eyeing Michelle suspiciously.

What about this weather, eh?

Michelle It's hot.

Barry Hot? You're not kidding. It sure is hot. It's too hot. What can you do on a day like this? Nothing. Sweltering. Hot. Day. Hot day.

Michelle I see you made it.

Barry Made what?

Michelle It.

Barry It?

Michelle Here. It. Here. You made it here.

Barry I'm always here. I mean, I came today especially, but I'm always here. During the day at least. It's all the bams when it gets dark, isn't it?

Michelle Yeah. I hate bams. They should be sterilised.

Barry Is that why you hate the school? Bams?

Michelle No. Teachers.

Barry Teachers.

Michelle Higher results next week. Sorry, I bet you're sick of hearing about it.

Barry Yeah.

Michelle Still, you must have passed some this time.

Barry Thanks, Michelle. That's a great help.

Michelle I passed my standard grades.

Barry I passed my Standard Grades, a monkey could pass Standard Grades. Jesus. Sorry, Michelle, I didn't . . .

Michelle There was a monkey on *Reporting Scotland* that passed Higher Modern Studies.

Barry Well, I didn't. I didn't pass it first time and I bloody bet I didn't pass it the second time.

Michelle Did you get anything first time?

Barry A postcard. That's all they send you if you fail everything. From the SQA with love. Who wants their postie to know their results before they do? Seriously?

Our postman's got this big moustache and he smokes a cigar. Do you know the one? Big Mac? He wears like a cowboy hat and shorts all year round.

So last year he hands me the post and he fixes me with a look like a doctor saying you've got the leukaemia or something.

He says – (*adopts American accent*) 'I'm sorry, partner.'

I'm not shitting you. Would an envelope be too much to ask?

I'd like a look at that postie's CV. I bet he's been in prison. 'Sorry, partner.' Jeeso.

Michelle So no Highers?

Barry I don't know. They're not in yet. I might have got some this time.

Michelle That's a better attitude. Stick up for yourself. You know you're dead brainy. Brainy Barry. It's like your dad says about the standardised testing.
  You've no girlfriend though, have you?

Barry No.

Michelle Good. So what are we going to do on our date?

Barry Is this a date?

Michelle I think so.

Barry Like Americans go on?

Michelle Yes. But no bowling. Bowling sucks.

Barry Right.

Michelle So what are we going to do?

Barry Right. I hadn't thought.

Michelle You're lucky I did.

Barry So what are we going to do?

Michelle We're going to hang about the wall for a little while.

  Pause.

Barry So have you got any plans for the holidays?

Michelle I plan to take over the world, I plan to burn down the school. I plan to write a novel about a pretty fifteen-year-old arsonist and her plans to take over the world.
  Do you really want to talk about plans? Don't you want to hear what happens on the rest of our date?

Barry You had me at 'hang about the wall'.

Michelle We're going to walk.

Barry Where are we going to walk?

Michelle We'll walk through the park. I expect you'll want to tell me how pretty I am.
  I might let you hold my hand.

Barry What way do we walk?

Michelle We take the high road up the bank. We're shielded from view by the gorse bushes and it feels like we're the only people in Stewarton. You tell me a secret you've never told anyone.

Barry Do you tell me a secret?

Michelle Sort of.

Barry Sort of?

Michelle I tell you it's a secret, but it isn't really. Boys can't keep secrets.

Barry So what else happens on our date?

Michelle I know what you want to know. I'm surprised at you, Barry, it's our first date.

Barry I didn't . . . I really didn't mean that. God, Michelle, I'm sorry . . . I wouldn't, I couldn't, I . . . I'd never expect to . . .

Michelle Relax. I'm joking. We go to my house.

Barry Is your mum in?

Michelle I thought you liked my mum?

Barry That's why I'm asking, is your mum in?

Michelle Barry you've got a one-track mind.

Barry It's not that. *It's not that.* Honestly, Michelle, it's just frightening or embarrassing or whatever seeing your mum. In these circumstances. I didn't mean . . . it's not about sex.

Michelle Sex? *Sex*, Barry Gordon? It's our first date, you're not even taking me bowling. You're a dirty degenerate.

Barry Oh my God, sorry, Michelle, I'm just saying the wrong thing, I don't expect anything, I know this is our first date or the first time we've seen each other or whatever . . . Look, can we start again? This isn't how I imagined . . . what I wanted . . .

Michelle I'm joking.

Barry What? God, stop fucking with me . . .

Michelle My mum's away looking at my Aunt Alice's new bungalow. She'll be there all night. She's there every night just now.

Barry You've got an empty?

Michelle I've got an empty.

Michelle leans forward and kisses him.

SCENE THREE

Tuesday evening: the wall.
  Norma and Rab.

Norma You stoled it.

Rab I didnae.

Norma You stoled it.

Rab I didnae.

Norma You stoled it.

Rab I didnae. You stole it.

Norma I didnae.

Rab You stole it.

Norma I didnae.

Rab You stole it.

Norma I didnae mean to. I wish I hudnae. I want tae put it back. But you stole it, Rab.

Rab I didnae, Norma. I presciently kenned you'd experience this change of heart. I'm keeping it safe fur you.

Norma I need it back. I need tae put it back. If my dad finds out, I'm dead.

Rab See. I kenned you'd be like this. I'm just hawding it for you, Norma. You can have it back any time you want.

Norma Can I have it back, Rab?

Rab No right this minute, Norma, no.

Norma Please, Rab. Please. I need to put it back before he notices.

Rab I cannae help you the night, Norma, I'm a man on a mission. Meet me here the morrow and I'll gie you it back then.

Norma Nae pish?

Rab Nae pish.

Norma Is that Barry coming roon the Monkey Trail?

Rab Looks like it.

Norma Don't say anything to him, Rab.

Rab Beat it and stop nippin ma heid, then. I'll see you tomorrow.

Norma Promise?

Rab Swear on the centre circle at Ibrox.

> *Norma exits. Rab is alone. Barry enters. He sits on the wall next to Rab. He drinks from a Panda Cola bottle containing a flat red liquid. Both are silent until Rab starts theatrically sniffing and twitching his nose.*

Sniff sniff. Haw haw. The big man's got a sneaky carry out. What you drinking, big man?

Barry A mixture.

Rab A mixture of what?

Barry It's a mixture of loads of different stuff from my old man's cupboard.

Rab Your dad's quality, man, Gordon Gordon. It's a pure mixture? How's it red?

Barry I have to be careful what I take, it can't be anything he drinks too often or he'd get sus. He doesn't drink the red stuff.

Rab What is the red stuff?

Barry Sometimes it's Campari but they've got hunners of half-drunk red booze. I don't think red is a very popular colour for booze. I don't mind though, it all tastes the same to me, so whenever I'm making up a mixture I start off with a third of red stuff and top it up with whisky, gin, vodka, Madeira . . . just whatever.

Rab Can I get a drink?

Barry No.

Rab How no?

Barry It's scientific, Rab. I've got just enough in this wee Panda Cola bottle to get me buckled but if I give you a drink I'll no get buckled. And you'll no get buckled off one swally and then neither one of us will be buckled. And no one wants that, Rab.

Rab thinks.

Rab If you gie's a swally I'll gie you half my Buckie when I get it.

Barry Where are you getting Buckie?

Rab Shop.

Barry How are you getting Buckie from I. D. Iqbal? You look about twelve.

Rab His daughter's working tonight. I heard him say.

Barry So?

Rab So . . . me and Veera Iqbal are hot and heavy.

Rab does over-animated shagging mime involving wildly uncoordinated pelvic thrusts.

Barry Fuck off, what age is she? Fourteen? That's jailbait. She's the same age as my wee sister.

Rab Your Norma's a wee lassie, Veera Iqbal is a doll. Are you saying you wouldnae? I'd put her on a pedestal – (*beat*) and look up her skirt.

Barry You know what they call that, Rab? Statutory rape. It's against the law.

Rab It isnae statutory rape. It's indecent assault. In this country. Statutory rape's America. They'll no prosecute you if you're just a wean too but.

Barry Rab, you're sixteen.

Rab Aye a ken, fourteen-year-olds wouldnae shag me if I was fourteen, would they? Sixteen-year-olds wilnae. Sixteen, seventeen, fourteen, fifteen, what's the difference anyhow?

Barry Sixteen's legal. Tony Blair'd give you the Johnny bags himself.

Rab He's a fucking dobber anyway. So are you gieing me a drink or what?

Barry I told you, it's all measured. It's scientific.

Rab Science my arse.

Barry You just don't have a thirst for knowledge, Rab.

Rab I've got a thirst, gie's a swally.

Rab snatches the bottle out of Barry's hand, takes a big slug then spits it out in disgust.

That's boggin'.

Barry I told you you didn't have a thirst for knowledge. Give me it back, you're getting slevers all in it.

He hands it back, spitting all the time.

Rab You're a weird guy, by the way.

Barry Coming from you, I'll take that as a compliment.

Rab Even if Veera disnae gie me the Buckie, I'll just take it. You know what they'll say? 'There's been a Rabbery. Oh no, we've just been Rabbed. It's the Rabbery of the century.'

Rab collapses in laughter at his joke.

Barry I have to say, Rab, I'm surprised at you and Veera.

Rab Oh aye? How's that?

Barry Well, you know . . .

Rab Aye?

Barry Well, I wouldn't have thought . . .

Rab Aye?

Barry Well, you're a ned, Rab.

Rab I prefer bam.

Barry Aye, you're a bam and she's Asian.

Rab All bam's are racist, is that it, Barry? That's racist, you're racist, racist against bams. Don't get me wrong, I am aware there are cultural differences. I'd be naive to think otherwise – know what I mean? But it's no like we can danner about with some narrow, specific ideal of who we want to hook up with. Best we can hope for in this short burl roon life is to find someone we connect with and find attractive, and they can put up wie oor miserable puss. You do that and you're ahead of the game.

'F you hing roon waiting oan a tall, athletic ginger-haired girl who loves the Rangers and enjoys group sex you'll be waiting a long time.

'S like fishing for salmon in a trout loch.

The van chimes play.

Barry That's the van coming.

Rab I might not get the Buckie anyway now. Fuck hanging about with you, Barry man, this is dead boring. I might just get some crebs from the van and go home an' play some Championship Manager.

Barry drains the bottle. Michelle enters.

Michelle How are you?

Barry I'm OK, thanks.

Michelle What are you doing?

Barry Just chilling, you know how it is.

Michelle Chilling? Should I leave you alone to 'chill' in peace?

Barry No, no don't. Two can chill.

Michelle There's already two of you.

Barry Rab was just going.

Rab Aw zat how it is, Barry man? Fuck this, man, I am just going up the house.

Rab exits.

Michelle How are you?

Barry Great. I'm really great. How are you?

Michelle I'm OK.

Pause.

Barry *and* **Michelle** I'm sorry.

Barry What are *you* sorry for?

Michelle You know.

Barry But that's why I'm sorry.

Michelle I'm sorry, Barry. I do want to. It was all just. A bit early.

Barry That's why I'm sorry.

Michelle What?

Barry I was a bit early. I tried not to but it all just came gushing –

Michelle No! That's not what I meant.

Barry God. But sorry. You know. About your jeans.

Michelle It doesn't matter.

Barry I. Em. I don't have much experience. With girls. That girl on holiday was made up.

Michelle What girl on holiday? You never told me about a girl on holiday.

Barry I made her up.

Michelle I don't have much experience with boys either, Barry.

Barry I wasn't saying . . . I mean . . .

Michelle I'm not a slag.

Barry I know. I mean. I know. I'm not . . .

Michelle Relax.

Barry Anyway. It's better we didn't. Because you're still too young.

Michelle I'm not.

Barry You're fifteen.

Michelle So?

Barry That's too young.

Michelle According to who?

Barry The government.

Michelle I'm going to be sixteen on Sunday . . . *I'm mature.*

> *Barry leans over the wall and starts being violently sick.*

Michelle You're disgusting. *That's* disgusting. I'm not kissing you after that. And I've got another empty tonight.

Barry Just give me a minute.

He retches.

Michelle I'm going home.

Barry Hold on.

He retches more.

Michelle You're bogging, Barry.

Michelle exits. Barry wipes his face and runs after her.

Barry Michelle – wait up, Michelle.

Barry exits. Rab enters. He carries a tenpenny mix-up.

Rab Penny mix-ups. Fucking penny mix-ups, man.

He acts out his conversation with Veera Iqbal.

'Can I help you, Rabert?'
   'Emm uh emm uh emm . . . Uh, can I just get a tenpenny mix-up please, Veera.'
   Penny mix-ups. Fucksake, man!

Norma enters.

Norma Rab, Rab, my da's fun oot. My da's fun oot.

Rab Hawd the bus, Norma – where's the fire?

Norma My dad's going mental.

Rab How?

Norma He-knows-I've-tooked-his-hash-except-he-
disnae-know-I-took-it-he-thinks-Barry-took-it-which-
is-actually-worst-cos-he's-doing-his-nut-at-Barry-no-
meee . . .

Rab Slow doon.

Norma He says he's 'betrayed the sacred trust between
father and son' and he says he cannae huv Barry living in
the house any more because he would never feel happy
going out again.

Rab So where's the problem? You're in the clear.

Norma He says he's a 'lazy wee bastard' and he's no got a 'moral centre'. He's pure beeling, Rab, you're gonna need tae get me the hash back now. I cannae let Barry –

Rab I really don't understand your consternation, Norma. Barry's big enough to take one for the team.

Norma Piss off, Rab. I cannae let Barry take the blame.

Rab Right – what's the worst thing at'll happen if Barry takes the blame? Your da'll gie him a bollocking but then it'll be all forgotten, no harm done – Barry's seventeen. He's a man, man.

Norma R–a–ab!

Rab If you hand it in and spill your guts but, then you'll get papped off tae a fucking counsellor or rehab or some shit – you're only fourteen, Norma, your folks'll think you'll be jagging up by the time you're fifteen. Least you can hope for is an Ayrshire intervention.

Norma What?

Rab A kicking and a kidnapping.

Norma Don't, give's it.

Rab That's what I'm saying. I won't give you it. Better all round.

Norma FUCK OFF, RAB!

Rab Right, fine. I'll get you it back.

Norma Now?

Rab No right the now, but as soon as I can. Do you want a tenpenny mix-up?

He inspects the contents of his mix-up.

Actually it's more like an eightpenny mix-up now – I cannae resist a Pink Shrimp.

Barry enters.

Norma BARRY!

Barry (*mimics her urgent tone*) NORMA! You're out awfully late.

Rab Right then, I'll see youse round.

Norma I mean it, Rab.

Rab Aye, aye. Catch youse.

Rab exits.

Barry What's up?

Norma Barry, you need to come home now, Dad's going spare.

Barry This night just gets better and better . . .

Norma Barry, you need to come home *now*! Dad's going to come and get you if you don't. He's going spare.

Barry What have I done now?

Norma . . . I don't know, but serious, Barry, you better come home now or he'll come down here looking for you. He's pure raging.

Barry Fuck him, Norma, he'll be all stoned and he'll have worked himself up about something that's nothing. I'm sick of him.

Norma Barry . . .

Barry I'm sick of him going on about the Female Eunuch while my mum's doing all the cleaning, washing and cooking and she's goat a job.

Norma Teaching isnae a job, it's a vocation.

Barry Aye, so he says, what's his vocation? Channel 5? Scratching his arse? He's like a fucking Arab sheikh, man. Has that arsehole ever had a job? Not as long as I remember.

It's his fault we've always had shit trainers, Norma. Nicks, Roebock, Addidad. If he had worked a day in his life maybe we could have had a real pair . . .

Norma But then we'd have been part of the capitalist-consuming machine.

Barry God Almighty we are. We are. WE ARE. You may as well say you don't want to be part of the oxygen-consuming machine. You've no choice in the matter. Claiming benefits doesnae make you a socialist.

Norma *Barry.*

Barry I'm sick . . .

He is sick.

I'm sick of putting his line on on a Saturday and then listening to him fucking moaning about how shite Kilmarnock are when he's spent twelve quid on the line and he hasnae been tae a match since Willie Waddle won the league. I'm sick of his big fat face and his big fat arse and his big fat opinions about everything. I'm sick of everything about him, Norma.

Norma Please, Barry, please go and see him. Just sort it out. You'll be affronted if he comes doon here in one of his moods.

Barry You'll be affronted.

Norma So? Barry, neither of us wants him out in public.

Barry I can take a beemer better than a fucking lecture, Norma. And anyway, I'm pissed.

Norma Please, Barry, please just go home and sort it out. He's scaring me.

Barry I cannae, Norma. I'll make it worse.

Norma It cannae get any worse, he's kicked your bedroom door in and he's filling bin bags with your stuff.

Barry Do you really want the drunk cavalry?

Norma Please, Barry.

Barry I can never refuse a damsel in distress, especially when it's my favourite girl. Come on, wee yin, let's go and listen tae Daddy's pish, then. Actually, give's a minute and I'll get rid of the rest of my carry-out.

Barry retches behind the wall. He composes himself and they begin to exit together.

Norma I love you, Barry.

Barry I'm the one that's pissed, Norma.

Norma I know, I just want you to know that I love you.

Barry I'm a big brother. We're there to take the shit for you. We take the shit so you don't have to.

Norma I do love you, though, I really mean it.

Barry Anything you need, it's all part of the service. (*Beat.*) No piggybacks, but, cos I'm all pissed and I'll drop you.

They leave the stage.

SCENE FOUR

Later Tuesday evening: the wall.
    Barry enters crying. He has a bloody nose. Norma runs after him.

Norma No way. No way would Dad hit you. No way. Barry, I'm sorry, Barry. I'm sorry.

Barry Not your fault.

Norma It is.

Barry Not your fault he's a fucking animal.

Norma He's not an animal. You don't understand.

Barry I go in. He's there with the fucking bin bag in his hand. 'Where have you been?' he says, really calm and reasonable. I tell him I've been with Michelle and he says 'Michelle who?' and I tell him and he repeats it like he can't believe it and I say, 'I was with Michelle Montgomery, what's it to you?' His voice changes and it's like when Gran died and he asks me if she's my girlfriend and I say 'No, she's helping me fill in my UCAS form,' and he fucking hit me, Norma, full strength, he hit me full strength. It's not like he slapped me or cuffed me or belted me. He hit me. He's got something wrong with his brain, he snapped like a schizo.

Norma Dad's no a spaz.

Barry He's a fucking loser and a lunatic and I swear, Norma, if he ever tries to hit me again I'll fucking kill him.

Barry paces.

Norma Barry, you don't understand.

Barry It's you that doesn't understand. Look, Norma, there's nothing you could say which will change anything. Me and him are over.

Norma Barry . . .

Barry Norma, I'm serious.

Norma But Barry . . .

Barry Go home, Norma.

Norma How can I go home? Dad's beeling and Mum's hysterectical.

Barry And do you think you being down the park at this time's going to help? They'll think you're getting paedo'd.

Norma starts to cry.

Norma Barry . . .

Barry comforts her.

Barry Right. I'll walk you to the end of the street, but I'm not going any closer than that.

Michelle enters. She is upset.

Michelle We need to talk.

Barry You go home, Norma.

Norma Barry, I need to tell you something.

Barry Home. Now.

Norma Barry.

Barry Norma. Home. I mean it.

Norma There's something I need to tell you.

Barry It doesn't matter. Whatever it is. It's Stewarton, Norma. Everything is always OK in the end.

Norma exits.

I'm sorry, Michelle. I'm sorry I'm a bit pissed. It's the holidays. I didn't know I'd be seeing you. We didn't have plans. I mean, I thought . . .

Michelle Barry, stop.

Pause.

Barry.

Barry What?

Michelle Something terrible has happened.

Barry What?

Michelle What's wrong with your face? Have you been fighting?

Barry Nothing, I just fell over. What's terrible?

Michelle We're moving.

Barry What?

Michelle I'm going away.

Barry What?

Michelle We're . . . me and my mum . . . *and Aunt Alice* . . . we're going away. Soon.

Barry A holiday? That doesn't matter. We can text. Phone. Email.

Michelle No. Going away. We're moving. We're moving away. Stewarton's suffocating us, Mum says. Says we're like a butterfly in a jam jar.

Barry You're flitting?

Michelle We're flitting.

Pause.

Barry I knew it. I knew it. I knew it. Nothing good ever happens to me.

Michelle God, Barry – are you sure you're OK? You're bleeding.

Barry How could I ever have a girlfriend? How could a girl ever like me? A girl like you. Like me.

Michelle I do like you.

Barry You know when you tell a joke and no one laughs? That's what it's always like for me . . .

Michelle But I do like you.

Pause.

Barry I love you.

Michelle It's only been three days.

Barry But the holidays are like a microwave.

Michelle Barry . . .

Barry I need you, Michelle. I know it's only been days, I know that, I know it's stupid, I know that, but I need you, Michelle.

Michelle I really am sorry. It's so . . . It's so . . . It's so . . . unfair. You've been the best boyfriend I've had.

Barry Better than Bennett McBride? Cheers, Michelle. He's got a lazy eye.

Barry leans over the wall and retches.

Michelle He doesn't have a lazy eye.

Barry continues retching.

Barry He wears a patch.

Michelle It's a special pair of glasses. And he didn't wear them when . . . forget it. I'm sorry, Barry.

Barry finishes retching and wipes his face.

Barry This is so stupid. Butterfly up my arse.

Michelle We need to be somewhere more liberal. More broadminded. Less *Daily Record*. Apparently. Whatever that means. She says we need to move now. To avoid disrupting school.

I mean . . .
FUCK SCHOOL.

Barry But if you're going away, who's running the
health-food shop?

Michelle Dixon McCurdie.

Barry The butcher?

Michelle How many Dixon McCurdies do you know?

Barry This is shite, just shite, Michelle. You. And me.
You felt it, didn't you? It wasn't just me?

Michelle Barry . . .

Barry It's like I've won the lottery but my mum's put the
ticket through the wash.

Michelle I felt it.

Barry My mate Stove told me this would be the best
summer ever. Left school, no responsibilities, nothing but
time and sunshine he said. This is a shite summer.

Michelle I felt it too, Barry. I did.

Barry Where are you going?

Michelle It doesn't matter. Too far.

Barry Where?

Michelle Why does it matter?

Barry Where?

Michelle Why?

Barry I just want to know to which far-off fortress of
solitude my love is being taken by the forces that conspire
against us.

Beat.

Michelle Barassie.

SCENE FIVE

Sunday: the wall.
  Barry is alone.

Barry I miss her mascara on my T-shirt. I miss those wee skirts. I miss those wee skirts because they showed me her legs. I miss her legs. I miss her arse. I miss her.

I wake up in the morning and she's the first thing I think about. Before I'm even conscious of my own identity, I'm aware of her. I'm in love with, her.

She's put me off my reading. And my food. Norma's worried I'm becoming anoraktic. Before Thursday I had only used about ten per cent of my available emotions. I'm not sure I like the other ninety.

I went to Barassie yesterday. It just all seemed so stupid, so melodramatic, like something out a book. Her being sent away. Turns out it isn't that far. But it turned out going to Barassie was stupid because I didn't know where she was. Or what I'd say if I saw her. So I just wandered along the shore.

The point is I only saw her for three days.

She's like an unanswered question.

  Pause.

My sister, I nearly slept with – the unanswered question.

  End of Act One.

Act Two

Sunday morning: Barassie shore.
  Michelle is alone.

Michelle Sixteen. What use is being sixteen in Barassie?
  It's like he's a paedophile or a Tory or in Iraq or dead.
I'm not even allowed to mention his name in front of her.
And I only talk to her. Them. The lesbians. They didn't
mind Bennett McBride. He had a lazy eye and he didn't
have lazy hands and they didn't mind him.
  It sounds stupid. I hate people who say things like this,
but it felt like we'd met before. Not that exactly because
we must have, because Stewarton's like that. But there was
something. A something . . . a connection. An energy.
  God. I just said 'energy'.
  The only way I can describe it. I hate folky, hippy
music. (*Beat.*) They love it. Joan Baez makes me want to
fill my ears with cement. It's all such whiney shit. The
first time I heard *Blue* by Joni Mitchell though, it was
different. It was like I already knew all the tunes. The
words almost. I *loved* it. But it wasn't like hearing a new
record. It wasn't like the first time I heard Nirvana. It
was better than Nirvana. It was like it was already in my
DNA. It was like I was hearing it again. (*Beat.*) And then
she said she'd played it a lot when she was pregnant.
That must be why, I must have remembered it from
before I was born. It must be the first album I'd ever
heard. But I definitely hadn't heard it since because she
only had it on vinyl. The way I felt the first time I heard
Blue. That's how I feel about him. About Barry. That's
how I felt when he started talking to me at the wall. Like
it made total sense for us to be there, together, talking.

43

And I want to tell her that, I want to tell her I'm in love and I want us to talk about it. I want her to tell me that's how it was with my dad and that she's happy for us. I want to talk about my dad. I've never asked. I've never needed more family before, but I want to know now. I want to know now.

I thought I saw him yesterday on the beach, I got excited, then I realised it wasn't him. Couldn't be him.

It's only Sunday. It's only been five days, but it feels like a whole term of school.

Sings sadly.

Happy birthday to me,
Happy birthday to me,
Happy birthday, dear Michelle,
Happy birthday to me.

SCENE TWO

Sunday afternoon: the wall.
Rab and Norma.

Rab Sunday's pure shite.

Norma 'S not. T4's on. *Friends* and the OC and that.

Rab That's shite, Norma.

Norma 'S not.

Rab Why're you no home watching it, then?

Norma No telly in my room.

Rab No telly in your room? That's child abuse, Norma.

Norma Dad says it rots your brain. Dulls your cognitive faculties.

Rab God, your dad's a pure prick. Can you no watch it in your lounge or something?

Norma It's shocking at home, Rab.

Rab Change the record. I'm going to get you the hash back, I says. Even God gives it a rest on a Sunday, Norma.

Pause.

Norma I think that Michelle Montgomery's pregnant.

Rab Haw haw, old Barry slipped one past the goalie? Nice one, man, you're going to be an auntie and you huvnae even grown tits.

Norma Fuck off, Rab, I do so have tits.

Rab That's aw bra, Norma.

Norma Anyway, I'm serious. I think they've taken her to a convent. In Barassie.

Rab I thought June Montgomery was a Buddhist.

Norma They've got Buddhist convents. I seen them on the TV. They're aw baldy and they wear orange goons and bathies.

Rab I don't see Michelle Montgomery wearing an orange goon. Maybe they've gone to a satanic convent.

Norma I'm serious, but. You don't get took away from home for winching. And my mum and dad are fighting all the time now. I've asked my dad and he says there's nothing going on. My mum just cries or shouts. And Barry wilnae even talk to anyone. Someone's going to have to tell me what's wrong – it's serious, Rab.

Rab Lighten up, Norma, you're on your holidays. Families are murder. You can choose your friends but you cannae choose your family. Except I've always thought

45

that's a load of bollocks, cos you cannae choose your friends either. I mean, I always thought me and Barry Ferguson would get along but do you see me phoning him up for a wee drink and to go bamming up some Tims? Naw. Because it's just whoever life throws your way.

It's like we live in Stewarton, right? An' so our pals all come from Stewarton an' they were probably in our class at the Robertland or live on the same street or whatever.

Norma That's Stewarton. It's a village. The world's outside Stewarton.

Rab Aye, that'll be right. Say I'm wan o' they socially mobile cunts in Glasgow, nice flat in the West End, good job, went tae uni. Do you think he chose his friends? Did he fuck, I bet they went tae uni wie him or work wie him or go to the same yoga class or maybe the wife's introduced them but he hasnae chose them. Has he fuck, it's the best of a bad bunch and that's all friends are, Norma. And families? No even the best. Just a bad bunch.

Norma She isnae family. Just cos she's Barry's girlfriend. It isn't family.

Rab Don't worry, Norma. It'll aw blow over and you'll be pure raging you wasted your summer worrying about nothing. Why don't you go up the Ducky and see if anyone's swimming?

Norma Eww, swimming up the Ducky's minging.

Rab Exactly, it's pure funny watching aw the wee fannies come out covered in brown sludge.

Norma My mum says you get the plague out the Ducky.

Rab The plague?

Norma Aye, you get it out rat shite. Are you going up the Ducky?

Rab Eh, no the now, Norma, no. I'll get you up there. I'm going to the shop.

Norma I'll come wi you.

Rab Eh naw, you're alright, pal.

Norma I don't mind.

Rab Naw, it's no that, Norma.

Norma What is it?

Rab Eh. I need to see Veera.

Norma I'll come, she's in my PE class. She disnae have tae dae it, though. Cos she's an Islam. Lucky cow.

Rab It's kind of personal.

Norma How's it personal? (*Beat.*) Oh.

Rab Aye, well . . . I'd better jazz.

Norma Are you going out wi Veera Iqbal?

Rab Aye.

Norma How's she never said anything to me?

Rab Well, we're no exactly going out . . . more seeing each other.

Norma What's the difference?

Rab Alright, we're not going out but the next time you see us we will be.

Norma Are you going to ask her out the now?

Rab Aye.

Norma Just like that?

Rab Aye.

Norma How?

Rab I just took a notion to Norma, and I'm a man of action, as you know.

Norma That's not what I meant. I meant how are you going to ask her out?

Rab Because I like her. I think there's a wee bit of magic between us.

Norma No, *how* are you going to ask her out?

Rab Is it cos I'm asking her out and no you? Are you a wee bit jealous, Norma?

Norma No, *how*! What are you going to say?

Rab I don't know. 'Howzabout it, Veera doll'?

Norma Have you never asked a girl out before, Rab?

Rab Who asks people out? You meet down the wall on a Friday or Saturday and start winching. It's Stewarton, no *Sex and the City*.

Norma But you're going to ask Veera out?

Rab She disnae go down the wall.

Norma Well, at least think about what you're going to say.

Rab Aw, if I think about it any more ma heid's gonna burst. I'll see you later, Norma. Oh noh. Now I'm nervous. Jeeso, Norma, if I bottle it and end up buying aw crebs and Johnny bags again I'm blaming you.

Rab exits.

Norma Wait, wait, Rab. What aboot the hash?

Norma begins singing:

'The people's flag is deepest red,
It shrouded oft our martyred dead . . .'

48

Barry enters.

Barry Why are you singing that, Norma?

Norma Barry.

Barry Why are you singing that?

Norma Reminds me of being wee. I hated being wee, but being big is shite. I'm so sorry, Barry, I really didn't mean . . .

Barry Doesn't matter.

Norma It does, but. You alright, Barry?

Barry No. No, I'm not, Norma.

Norma D'you wanna talk?

Barry I don't, Norma. I can't. Could you just go somewhere else, please?

Norma Where?

Barry Please?

Norma Where?

Barry I don't know. The Chooky Brae? The Digital? The swings? The Ducky? I don't care, Norma. I'm sorry, I'm no angry at you but I need to be on my own. Here. I need to be on my own here.

Norma dismounts the wall and begins to exit.

Norma You sure you don't want to talk, Barry?

Barry No.

Norma But I want to talk. There's something I need to tell you –

Barry Sorry, Norma. Not just now.

Norma Barry, I didn't mean to . . .

49

Barry Go. Away. Norma.

Norma You think I don't understand. You think I don't know about love. Well, I do, Barry. I know that I love you. And Mum loves Dad. And they both love both of us.

Norma begins to exit.

I know that real love's family.

SCENE THREE

Monday afternoon: the wall.
  Rab and Barry.

Rab *Fuck. Ing. Hell.*

Pause.

Right. Michelle Montgomery, June the lemon's daughter, is your sister?

Barry Yes.

Rab And your girlfriend?

Barry Yes. No. She was my girlfriend. She's gone. She's gone.

Rab Haw haw, all this time you've been bamming me up about being a paedo and your bird's yer sister. That's classic, man. You dirty beast. The *Daily Record*'ll be at your door.

Barry I am a beast, Rab. I know she's my sister now . . .

Rab How'd you know?

Barry He hit me when he heard we were going out. Socked me. He really socked me. Like in the *Batman* telly show. Sock!

Rab Aye – your da's a tank man.

Barry And my mum. God, Rab. It's killing my mum.

Rab Did she no ken like?

Barry No. I don't know. I mean. She said it was like when you're asleep and your alarm's beeping away but you just integrate it into your dream and ignore it, but then something happens and you're suddenly awake and aware your alarm has been going for ages.

When he hit me it all fell into place. And she had to tell me because. She. She didn't want me to do anything. You know. *Anything*.

Rab Haw haw. You dirty bastard, man.

Barry I know. I am.

Rab I know you are.

Rab That's just it, Rab. I know she's my sister, but that isn't how I see her. It's like I looked at her one way and that's the only way I can look at her. I know it's wrong, I am a beast but I can't help it, I still fancy her, I still want to ride her.

Rab Haw haw, Barry man, I amnae a psychologist, I don't know what to tell you, man. It's fucked up.

Pause.

I was watching this thing on the Discovery Channel the other day. These cunts right, they hud some monkeys, right, and they dehydrated them. Didnae gie them any water for like three days. Then the cunts offer them a choice, right, the monkeys can huv either a refreshing drink of their favourite juice or they can look at a picture of a lady monkey's arse. Juice or arse, right. You know what the stupid monkeys picked?

Barry The picture of the arse.

51

Rab The picture of the lady monkey's arse, man, that's priceless, the stupid wee monkeys wid rather have a wank and die of thurst than have a drink an no. We're aw monkeys, man, it's aw pure biological shite, you cannae help it. Way I see it, if we were oot in the jungle who cares she's your sister – know what I mean?

Barry She's my sister.

Rab I'm a libertarian, Barry, do what you want, live and let live. It's no my cup of tea, but then I've a brother. An' he's boggin'.

Barry She's my sister.

Rab Aye, you're right, man, you are a beast.

Pause.

I'm sure it'll pass, Barry man.

Pause.

It's gonna be weird now, but, at Christmas, knowing you've shagged your sister. 'Pass the sprouts.'

Barry I haven't. We didn't.

Rab Haw haw, beemer. That's more embarrassing, man, I wouldnae tell anyone that. What are you worrying about then, man, a wee kiss? I've done more than that wi' ma da, man.

Beat.

I havenae really though, ken.

Barry Exactly. We didn't really do anything, but then that's why I'm a beast, it could all be forgotten in a year, a wee misunderstanding rectified once I found out, and a normal relationship. As normal as you can have with a secret half-sister. It could be nothing but I still want to

52

fuck her, Rab, I still do. I'm not right, I'm like a fucking paedo or something, Rab, my brain's wired funny.

Rab Honestly, Barry, why are you telling me this? Shouldn't you talk to your dad or your mum or a priest or the Samaritans or some cunt? Or her? I'm mad Rab McGuire, mental bam an' ladies' man, I don't know what to tell you, by rights I should be gieing you nuclear pelters an getting an advert out in the *Kilmarnock Standard* telling everyone.

Barry So why don't you, why aren't you?

Pause.

Rab Honestly, man? This is all so fucked up I feel sorry for you. Wee Norma says it's like *EastEnders* round your house. It fucking sounds like it.

Barry Listen, Rab, there's something else.

Rab Christ, I don't want to hear it. Have you got knob rot? Baw cancer? Are you losing a limb?

Barry It's like I'm drowning. I'm sorry, I need to say it out loud, Rab, that's all. I need to say it out loud.

Rab Fucksake, go on, man, what is it?

Barry Ever since. Ever since I've known. All night. I keep repeating in my head, 'Barry committed suicide,' or like, 'Barry died,' or imagining my funeral and all the mourners and flowers and a grave. But mainly it's like, 'Barry died' and 'Barry committed suicide' over and over like a mantra.

Rab Shut up, Barry. Don't fucking kill yourself. Don't be so fucking stupid. What age are you – seventeen? You haven't lived, don't be such a fucking pussy, thinking about suicide over some crush, killing yourself over a bird. Don't be a fucking bawbag. Have you ever taken smack?

Barry No.

Rab Crack?

Barry No.

Rab Used a gun?

Barry No.

Rab Driven a car?

Barry No.

Rab Got your hole?

Barry Yes.

Rab Got your hole?

Barry No.

Rab Been to Alton Towers?

Barry No.

Rab Then there's so much more to live for. Or at the very least to do before you kill yourself.

Barry It's not like I am thinking about killing myself, it's just like I'm thinking how much easier it would be for everyone.

Rab Fuck them, let them look after themselves. It will be alright, Barry. It's your first summer after leaving school, man, you live in Stewarton, everything will be alright. Everything's alright in Stewarton.

Barry The fucking skies have opened up, Rab. Nothing is ever going to be the same again. It may as well be raining frogs.

Rab I'll tell you something else, Barry. The lady monkeys, right? They did the same experiment with them, right? They dehydrated those cunts an aw and they offered them the same choice, a drink of juice or a look at a male monkey's arse. What do you think the lady monkey's chose?

Barry I don't care.

Rab Aye, fucking whine on, you wee bitch. You're moping around like you have a fucking choice. You've fuck-all choice, there's no dilemma, all you can do is fucking forget it and move on. What you thinking? You'll elope and be together? They don't even let you marry your sister in Dunlop, man. Fucking get over it. Or pretend. Pretend you don't feel like that for long enough, it doesn't matter one way or the other how you actually do feel. Eventually you will forget her anyway, man. It will pass. I've never fancied a bird longer than a month, tops. I know it's a fucker but it'll happen anyway, so you may as well try and speed it up, don't fucking mope.

Barry Mope?

Rab Aye, or at least let me finish my fucking story, let me distract you from your self-pity for a wee minute.

Barry Go on.

Rab Well? What do you think the lady monkeys chose?

Barry The juice.

Rab Exactly, they're no fucking stupid, man.

Barry So you're saying I should –

Rab SHUT UP, MAN. This isnae about you, it's just the end of the fucking story about the monkeys the cunts dehydrated.

Barry Sorry.

Rab Aye, so the lady monleys arenae daft, they take the juice. It's cherry juice, by the way.

55

Barry Why cherry juice?

Rab I dunno, it's the lady monkeys' favourite. It's aw monkeys' favourite. So they took the juice. But then they did it again, the same experiment. They obviously dehydrated them again, or maybe they had different lady monkeys, naw that wouldnae be scientific, so aye, it was the same ones they dehydrated again. They did it again but instead of just a normal average male monkey's arse they offered them a picture of the dominant male's arse – he's like the big man, know what I mean?

Barry I know what the dominant male is.

Rab You got Discovery too, aye? So what do you think they did? They went for the fucking photae. Birds think they're so fucking superior, man, think we're superficial but they don't care, they only want the big dog. What do you think of that? They only want the big man, know what I mean? At least what a bird looks like is actually her, man – what's a job? Money? Fuck all, they're not you. Birds are fucking stupid, man.

Barry I don't understand what this has got to do with –

Rab Shut up for a minute. I've thought of something.

Rab is exceptionally pleased with himself.

Here, you know who you're like?

Barry Who?

Rab Out *Star Wars*?

Barry thinks.

Barry Luke Skywalker.

Rab Luke Skywalker. You know how?

Barry He fancied –

Rab He wanted tae fuck his sister, aye – Princess Leia. See, what you need to do is just what all men need to do, man. Be less like Skywalker and more like Solo. Han Solo – that's a good Protestant name, by the way.

Barry Han fancied Leia too . . .

Rab Aye, but she wasnae his sister, was she? Do you think Han Solo would be queering around gurning like a puss over some wee bird? Naw. Would he fuck.

Barry What am I meant to do, Rab?

Rab Well . . . I was on my way to ask out Veera Iqbal . . .

Barry I thought you two were hot and heavy.

Rab Aye, we will be. I'm a busy man, I huvnae had time, I *wuz* on my way tae ask her out. But. You know. I suppose in the circumstances. I mean. Come up the road wi' me for a game of Champo. Take your mind off it.

Barry Thanks, Rab.

Rab Aw, I'm going to pump you, man, don't thank me.

Michelle enters.

Barry Michelle!

Michelle Barry.

They embrace.

Rab Well, I'll leave youse to it then, droogs. Fucksake.

They are in a world of their own. Rab exits. They begin to kiss more and more urgently, passionately, until Barry pulls away, disgusted at himself.

Michelle What is it? What's wrong?

Barry I'm sorry.

Michelle What?

57

Barry is lost for words.

What is it, Barry?

Barry I'm . . . sorry. Really.

Michelle I love you.

Barry doesn't respond.

You love me.

Barry doesn't respond.

We're in love, Barry.

Barry No.

Barry starts to leave. Michelle grabs him. He pulls away.

Leave me alone. Just leave me alone. It's over.

Michelle It's only been days, Barry. What's happened?

Pause.

Barry People lie to each other, Michelle.

Michelle Why are you being like this? What's wrong?

Barry People lie to each other.

Michelle I know they do. Teachers lie to us. Our parents lie to us. But we don't lie to each other. I know you.

Barry You think you know me but you don't. You don't know anything.

Michelle Something's happened. I need to tell you something.

Barry What?

Michelle About my mum.

Barry Go on.

Michelle Can we just pretend we're the only people in Stewarton again?

Barry What is it?

Michelle It isn't. It isn't easy.

Barry Just tell me.

Michelle It's big. Changing. I mean, God. God, Barry.

Barry Please. I know.

Michelle You know?

Barry I mean. I think I know. Maybe. Maybe I know. Please just tell me what it is.

Michelle My mum . . .

Barry Yes?

Michelle My mum . . .

Barry Yes?

Michelle My mum's . . .

Barry What is it?

Michelle My mum's a lesbian.

Barry Is that it?

Michelle IS THAT IT?

Barry Sorry. I mean, I know. I thought you knew.

Michelle WHAT? Was it in the gay pages of the *Kilmarnock Standard*? How come you knew and I didn't?

Barry Stewarton's tiny. You can't keep a secret in Stewarton.

Michelle Turns out you can. We were moving to Barassie to be lesbians and I didn't even know. They lied to me.

Everything's a lie. Lesbians? I don't even know any lesbians.

Barry I . . .

Michelle And what happens now? My mum's a lesbian, my Aunt Alice is my stepdad and I live in Barassie. What happens now, Barry?

She cries.

Barry I'm sorry, Michelle. About your mum. And everything. I'm so sorry about everything.

Michelle I need you, Barry.

Barry I can't, Michelle.

Michelle So what's changed?

Barry Everything.

Barry starts to exit.

Michelle So you're just another liar, Barry Gordon? After all that you're just another liar?

Barry I'm really sorry. I just can't explain.

Michelle Well, just fuck you then. Fuck you and fuck my mum and fuck my aunt . . . fuck *Alice*. I'm sixteen now and I don't need any of you. All you lesbians and liars can just rot in Ayrshire.

Once Barry has gone Michelle emits a primal scream.

SCENE FOUR

Tuesday: the wall.
  Norma is bothering Barry.

Norma Highers tomorrow, Barry.

Barry doesn't respond.

I bet you do well.

Barry doesn't respond.

And once you get your Highers there's no stopping you.

Barry doesn't respond.

World's your osprey.

Barry doesn't respond.

Uni. Or college. Or a job. Or anything.

Barry doesn't respond.

Going to say something, Barry?

Barry sees Michelle.

Barry Michelle.

Michelle enters.

Norma I thought you were in Barassie.

Michelle Barassie's just two buses away. You change at Kilmarnock. Terminate at Avenue Square.

Norma Barry?

Barry I need to go.

Michelle I needed to see you.

Barry I can't.

Norma Barry, she got two buses.

Michelle I don't understand. What changed, Barry?

Norma What's going on?

Michelle I love you, Barry.

Barry Michelle –

Michelle Love like crucifixion. Like it's killing me. Like only you matter.

Norma Barry . . .

Michelle You know. You know how I feel. I know you do.

Barry I don't. I don't. I don't.

Norma You do. You've barely spoken or eaten or anything since she left.

Barry Norma, please.

Norma It's true. And she's taken two buses so . . .

Barry Norma, this is nothing to do with you.

Norma It is though, because you're to do with me.

Norma exits.

Barry Honestly. Please, just don't –

Michelle Just talk to me.

Barry You know those conversations you can never take back? The ones that change everything for ever?

Michelle I don't care. Whatever it is. I don't care. We're in love and that's more important than anything. That fixes everything.

Barry It doesn't fix anything. It makes everything worse.

Michelle Makes what worse? What does it make worse?

Barry Who's your father?

Michelle Why are you asking me that?

Barry It's important.

Michelle Why?

Barry Please. I need to know. Please just trust me.

Michelle My mum was young when she had me. He was gone when I was born. It doesn't matter. I don't have a dad. I've never had a dad. There's just some man somewhere and that's all. And that's not a dad.

Barry I'm sorry, Michelle.

Michelle It doesn't matter. I've never had a dad. I've never needed a dad.

Barry I don't know how to say it.

Michelle Say what?

Barry My dad.

Michelle What about your dad?

Barry He . . .

Pause.

He had an affair with your mum.

Michelle You said they went out. Him and Mum. They didn't. They didn't go out even. He was her teacher.

Barry He was what?

Pause.

Michelle He was my mum's teacher. They didn't go out. You said they went out, so I asked her before. Before all . . . this. They never went out even, Barry. She knows him because he was her teacher.

Barry I didn't know . . .

Pause.

I didn't know my dad was a teacher. My dad's not a teacher. He isn't a paedophile, he's a feminist.

Michelle I don't understand.

Barry My dad. Michelle. My dad. He's . . .

Michelle GOD. NO. No. That's not true. He isn't. NO! God, Barry. God. I feel sick.

Barry I'm sorry.

Michelle Say it.

   Barry can't.

Say it.

   Barry can't.

This is ruined. We're ruined. I'm ruined.

Barry Michelle . . .

   Michelle exits in tears.

SCENE FIVE

Wednesday: the wall.
   The stage is empty. Beat. Barry enters, pursued by Rab.

Rab Everything alright?

Barry Nothing.

Rab Highers the day, eh?

Barry Who cares?

Rab Has your sister said anything to you, Barry?

Barry What?

Rab Wee Norma, man. Keep up.

Barry What?

Rab Has she said anything?

Barry She never stops.

Rab Anything. Em. About me?

Barry Like?

Rab Right. Oh, nothing then. Disnae matter.

Barry Keep away from my sister.

Rab Oh, it's no like that, man, I've telt ye. Veera's the only one for me.

Barry Asked her out yet?

Rab I'm going . . . I'm on my way . . . I was just about . . . I've been . . . I meant to . . . *I'm going to ask her the now.* I AM! Fucksake. That's where I'm on my way to the now. Right fuck you. Watch this.

Rab exits. Barry is alone. Michelle enters.

Michelle Your dad broke my mum's heart.

Barry He's broken mine too.

Michelle He was her teacher.

Barry Michelle . . .

Michelle It isn't my mum's fault. I mean. They became friends. That can happen. He used to give her lifts to the Cumnock Communist Coalition meetings.

Barry Don't.

Michelle They fell in love.

Barry Please.

Michelle But they never acted on it, Barry. He was her teacher. They stopped seeing each other. Nothing happened. But then your mum found out.

Barry And?

Michelle You were a baby.

Barry I know. God, Michelle –

Michelle She told my granny.

Barry Minnie Malloy?

Michelle And that's when your dad lost his job.

Barry Oh God. I feel sick.

Michelle And that's when she met my dad.

Barry What?

Michelle She met my dad.

Barry Your dad?

Michelle Yes.

Barry Who is your dad?

Michelle You won't believe me.

Barry I believe you.

Michelle You won't. I know you won't.

Barry Oh my God. Not . . .

Michelle What? Not who?

Barry Dixon McCurdie?

Michelle NO!

Barry Then who? It's important, Michelle.

Michelle He was a roadie.

Barry He was what?

Michelle He was a roadie. She met him at a concert.

Barry What concert?

Michelle Is that really relevant?

Barry Sorry.

Michelle Iron Maiden.

Barry What?

Michelle Iron Maiden. The 'Bring Your Daughter to the Slaughter' tour.

Barry Do you believe that?

Michelle Yes. I mean. I don't know. But he can't. I mean. You're not . . .

Barry Your brother.

Michelle He isn't. This isn't. God. God, Barry. She would have told me that. She would have told me that.

Barry I'm so sorry, Michelle. About everything. I'm sorry.

Michelle I didn't know she was a lesbian. If she can lie to me for sixteen years . . . If she can lie to me for sixteen years about that, then I don't know what to believe. Barry, I need you, please just kiss me.

Barry Listen to me, Michelle, I can't, we can't, we need to find out what the truth is. I believed my mum, I believe my mum. I mean . . .

Michelle Then just hold me.

Barry Hold you as what? A brother? A lover?

Michelle Just hold me.

They embrace.

Lost.

Barry What?

Michelle When we met you said I looked lost. I am lost, Barry. I was lost before and I'm lost now. I'm lost.

Barry I need to speak to my . . . to *him*. I need to speak to Gordon Gordon.

Michelle I'm lost. So just stay. Just stay with me.

Barry But I'm lost too.

They start to kiss.

Wait for me, Michelle. I'm going up my house.

Barry exits.

SCENE SIX

Wednesday night: the wall.
  Michelle is alone. Rab enters.

Rab Eh . . . Barry no here?

Michelle No.

Rab Eh . . . Norma no here?

Michelle No.

Pause.

Rab You got a minute then, hen?

Michelle I suppose.

Rab Right. So there's this girl.

Michelle Veera Iqbal?

Rab How do you ken that?

Michelle Barry's my . . .

Rab Aye? Good luck wi aw that, doll. So Veera. I love her, man.

Michelle I have to say I'm surprised at you and Veera.

Rab How?

Michelle Well . . . you're a ned.

Rab Fucksake. Ned? Ned, is it? I fucking hate that.
Radge. Ned. Pikey. Greb. Insidious wee words.
   You've found a way tae slag off the working class an
get away wie it. It's fucking disgusting, writing off people
wie this lazy shorthand – that when you scratch away at
it, is entirely aimed at the young poor.
   Well, I am young and I am poor. And I'm fabulous.
   Neds. It's like saying fucking 'jiggaboo' isnae offensive
tae black folk. An if I wis black folk, you'd be fawing
over yourselves kissing my black ass. Racist.
   You look at the black underclass in America, they're
wearing sportswear, they're causing trouble at nights in
gangs, they're drinking carry-outs and smoking weed and
causing a nuisance. Are they neds, Michelle?
   An cos you think I'm a fucking ned you think I'm a
loser? It's your boyfriend or your brother or whatever it is
hasnae got a Higher tae his name. I got my results the day.
   Six 'A's.
   They want me tae go Cambridge.
   What dae you think of that, ya moody pseudo-
intellectual fanny? I'm gonna be the only bam at
Emmanuel College, and you and Veera Iqbal and aw the
player-haters can get it squarely up you. I'm coming out
strong, dragging myself oot the ghetto like a boxer or a
hip-hopper or something, 'cept I'm using my brains.

   Pause.

An she gave me a stanner just looking at her, man.
   So there I was, man. Standing in front of the swadgers.
Pouring out my heart. *Braveheart* style. In comes old
Iqbal – he still husnae forgave me for taxing a packet of
Murray Mints in 1995, he starts saying, 'Empty pockets,
McGuire. You got the bad hand.'

Bad hand? Bad hand? I'll gie him the bad hand. So I says, 'Away tae fuck.'

An he says, 'Search-find-keep.'

Now I believe in the sanctity of search-find-keep, I've used it on enough first years, and I hudnae been nicking his swadgers so I lets him search me.

The hash though, Michelle. I'd forgotten the hash.

Michelle The hash?

Rab Hud it in my pocket, tae. Eh. Gie back . . . tae . . . wee Norma . . . so she could gie it tae her old man. Aye. Get Barry out the doghouse.

So he pulls it out my tracky bottoms and starts throwing an eppy. He's going ballistic, man, ballistic. Talking about the police. The police.

So he's pulling me out by my hood and Veera's just looking at me, and then as he drags me by the sanitary towels I shout out, 'So will you go wie me then, Veera?'

An' she says, 'Sorry Rabert. You are not an appropriate suitor.'

No an appropriate suitor. No an appropriate suitor. I'm the dominant male.

Well, get it up aw youse, because Rab McGuire, mental bam an' straight 'A's man, is a working-class hero.

Pause. Rab's mother calls him from offstage. She has a posh accent.

Mrs McGuire Robbie, Robbie, supper's on the pantry table. You know it's eight o'clock mass and you're meant to be giving a reading. I'll come down to that wall and get you.

Robert, it's pesto night!

Pause. Rab looks embarrassed and begins to exit.

Rab She just sounds posh. Tell Barry Mr Iqbal's got his da's weed.

Rab exits. Norma enters, clutching an envelope containing Barry's Higher results.

Norma You're back?

Michelle Yeah.

Norma You seen my brother?

Pause.

Michelle Yeah.

Norma You two going out again, then? You sort it out?

Michelle No. A bit. Sort of. I don't know.

Norma You pregnant?

Michelle NO! God . . .

Norma How'd you get took tae Barassie, then?

Michelle None of your business.

Norma How, is Barry aw weird?

Michelle It's nothing to do with you, Norma.

Norma He's my brother. No one loves him more than me.

Michelle Is that why you let him take the blame for stealing your dad's hash, then?

Norma is aghast.

Norma What?

Michelle You heard.

Norma You don't understand, but . . .

Michelle It's none of my business.

Norma   . . . It's none of your business.

Michelle I know it isn't.

Norma Please don't tell Barry, Michelle. *Please!* I didn't. I mean. I wanted. I mean, PLEASE, Michelle. Please don't tell him . . .

Michelle I won't. It's nothing to do with me. But don't you come down here and give me all your family-first bullshit, Norma Gordon. Honestly, I've had it up to here with family. Families are full of it. They're just there to let you down and make you feel guilty. Family's a lie you tell yourself so you don't feel so alone. But you are. We are. Alone. We're all alone, Norma, and no amount of birthday cards and dinners at the table can change that.

Norma I was going. I tried. I mean. I did, Michelle. I tried to tell him but . . . I do love Barry. I do. Our family *is* different. And. I mean. I just made a mistake . . .

Barry enters.

Barry. Barry, I'm sorry, Barry.

Barry What about?

Norma I'm sorry, Barry. I took his hash. Me, I took his hash. I'm sorry, Barry, I'm sorry I took it and I'm sorry I let you take the blame.

Barry What hash?

Norma That's why he hit you, Barry. I thought you took it all the time, I didn't think he'd notice another wee bit. I din't even smoke any, honest.

Barry GOD! God, Norma. God. I can't believe you're smoking hash. You're only fourteen.

Norma So? I bet you were smoking hash at fourteen.

Barry Don't.

Norma I won't.

Barry You shouldn't.

Norma I didn't.

I'm going to put it back. I was going to put it back. But Dad hasnae been out since so I've not been able to put it back, and then he found out and I couldnae put it back, and I'm sorry, Barry. It's my fault he hit you.

Barry It's his fault. He's fifty and he leaves drugs around for his fourteen-year-old daughter to find. It's his fault. That's his fault, hitting me is his fault, it's all his fault. You should have told me though, Norma.

Norma I'm sorry.

Barry I've done some shit things to you over the years and I've never apologised, so I don't expect you to. No more apologies, Norma. I'm your big brother. And now we're square for the tofu incident.

Norma Dad loves you, Barry.

Barry Hmph.

Norma He's never hit you before, has he?

Barry No.

Norma Well, just forgive him, give him another chance, I'll tell him I took it and he'll say he's sorry and everything will be alright.

Barry Leave it. Forget it.

Michelle Barry . . .

Norma What can I do, Barry?

Barry Nothing, it's nothing to do with you. You need to go home.

She doesn't move.

Go home, Norma.

And don't say a word about the hash. It'll no make anything better.

Norma hands him the envelope.

Norma Your results are in, Barry.

He looks at it.

You got an envelope.

Michelle Barry . . .

Barry puts the unopened envelope in his pocket.

Barry?

Barry kisses Michelle like the world is ending. She pulls away.

Is it alright?

Barry hesitates.
  Snap black.

The End.